WE GET ALONG

by
Alex Hall

Minneapolis, Minnesota

Credits

Images are courtesy of Shutterstock.com. With thanks to Getty Images, Thinkstock Photo, and iStockphoto. Cover – Monkey Business Images, america365, Barks. 2–3 – Studio Romantic. 4–5 – Rawpixel.com, PeopleImages.com – Yuri A. 6–7 – PeopleImages.com – Yuri A, Rawpixel.com. 8–9 – fizkes, gpointstudio. 10–11 – Kinga, goodluz. 12–13 – anek. soowannaphoom, Miljan Zivkovic. 14–15 – Ksenia Shestakova, KOTOIMAGES. 16–17 – caseyjadew, DGLimages. 18–19 – Tatyana Dzemileva, wavebreakmedia. 20–21 – Lopolo, Prostock-studio. 22–23 – Tint Media, Drazen Zigic.

Bearport Publishing Company Product Development Team

Publisher: Jen Jenson; Director of Product Development: Spencer Brinker; Editorial Director: Allison Juda; Editor: Cole Nelson; Editor: Tiana Tran; Production Editor: Naomi Reich; Art Director: Kim Jones; Designer: Kayla Eggert; Designer: Steve Scheluchin; Production Specialist: Owen Hamlin

Library of Congress Cataloging-in-Publication Data is available at www.loc.gov or upon request from the publisher.

ISBN: 979-8-89577-027-6 (hardcover)
ISBN: 979-8-89577-458-8 (paperback)
ISBN: 979-8-89577-144-0 (ebook)

© 2026 BookLife Publishing
This edition is published by arrangement with BookLife Publishing.

North American adaptations © 2026 Bearport Publishing Company. All rights reserved. No part of this publication may be reproduced in whole or in part, stored in any retrieval system, or transmitted in any form or by any means, electronic, mechanical, photocopying, recording, or otherwise, without written permission from the publisher. Bearport Publishing is a division of FlutterBee Education Group.

For more information, write to Bearport Publishing, 3500 American Blvd W, Suite 150, Bloomington, MN 55431.

CONTENTS

WE ARE CONNECTED 4

GETTING ALONG 6

BEING KIND 8

BEING POLITE 10

SHOWING SUPPORT 12

SHARING 14

TAKING TURNS 16

DISAGREEMENTS 18

STOPPING BULLIES 20

WHY IT IS GOOD TO GET ALONG 22

GLOSSARY 24

INDEX 24

WE ARE CONNECTED

The world is full of people. We are all connected in a **society**. Together, we can make sure everyone has what they need.

There are more than 8 billion people in the world.

WHAT COMMUNITIES ARE YOU PART OF?

Within our society there are many different communities. These are groups that share things in common. Some communities are connected by a language or religion. There are also communities formed by people who all like the same thing, such as a sport's team.

GETTING ALONG

We live and work alongside many people every day. Sometimes, it takes a group to get things done. Often, it's just more fun to do things with friends.

Can you think of a time when you worked in a group?

Getting along is an important part of working together. But it is not always easy. How can we learn to get along?

BEING KIND

Everyone has feelings. So, it is important to be kind. Thinking of how others are feeling is called **empathy**. This forms strong **relationships** and helps build communities.

You can have different kinds of relationships with different members of your community.

What is one way you have shown empathy?

How can you show empathy? Just think of what you might want someone to do if the same thing were to happen to you. Then, do that for them! Often, when we show others empathy, they will do the same for us.

BEING POLITE

It is important to have good **manners**. It shows **respect** for the people around us. How can we be polite?

There are different rules in different communities about what is polite.

When you ask someone for something, remember to say "please."

If someone gives you something, always say "thank you."

Learning how and when to say sorry is also an important part of being polite.

SHOWING SUPPORT

Our friends are part of our communities. These are people we like to spend time with. It can be really fun to play games, watch TV, or talk with friends.

How do you feel when you get support from a friend?

Friends also give us support. This can make hard things a little bit easier. Friends help cheer us up when we have a bad day. They may help us with a tricky homework problem.

SHARING

Getting along often means we have to share. We need to split things with others. This way, we can all get a chance to enjoy the same thing.

You may share something as small as your colored pencils or as big as your school.

WHEN WAS THE LAST TIME SOMEONE SHARED SOMETHING WITH YOU?

Sharing keeps things fair. It is also a kind way to show others we are thinking about them. What you want or need is important. But so is what they need or want.

TAKING TURNS

One way to share is to take turns. You let someone else do something while you wait. This can take patience.

> Patience is waiting for something without getting upset.

WHEN ELSE DO YOU NEED TO TAKE TURNS?

We might need to take turns to do something, such as go on the swings. We also need to take turns while talking. When it is not your turn to speak, it's important to listen to what others have to say.

DISAGREEMENTS

Getting along doesn't mean we always agree. But that's okay! We may fight over who gets to play with a toy first. But what we do next is important.

We often feel angry or upset when we **disagree** with others.

When we disagree, we still need to show respect. We can try to understand how the other person is feeling. Take turns listening and speaking. Then, work together to solve the problem.

STOPPING BULLIES

Some people do not try to get along. They may pick on others. When people say or do mean things over and over, it is called bullying.

Being bullied is never your fault.

Think of a grown-up you feel safe talking to.

Often, we need help to stop bullies. If you or someone you know is being bullied, tell a trusted grown-up. Things are more likely to get better with their help.

WHY IT IS GOOD TO GET ALONG

There are many ways to get along with one another. We can be polite, kind, and learn to share. Getting along creates strong relationships.

People who get along are often happy to be around one another. This makes our society a nice place to be. It is better when we are all connected!

GLOSSARY

communities groups of people who live together or share something in common

disagree to think differently about something

empathy an understanding for the feelings and experiences of another

manners things we do to be kind and polite around others

relationships the connections that people have with one another

respect a feeling that someone or something is good and important

society all the people who live in the same area and share the same laws

support help and encouragement

INDEX

bullying 20
communities 5, 8, 10, 12
disagreement 18–19
empathy 8–9
friends 6, 12–13
manners 10
polite 10–11, 22
relationships 8, 22
respect 10, 19
sharing 5, 14–16, 22
support 12–13